How to Deal with

Kids' Health™

ALLERGIES

Lynette Robbins

PowerKiDS
press™

New York

For Andrew Michael Smith

Published in 2010 by The Rosen Publishing Group, Inc.
29 East 21st Street, New York, NY 10010

First Edition

Editor: Joanne Randolph
Book Design: Kate Laczynski
Photo Researcher: Jessica Gerweck

Photo Credits: Cover, p. 1 © www.istockphoto.com/Izabela Habur; p. 4 James Darell/Getty Images; p. 6 Lenora Gim/Getty Images; p. 8 Yo/Getty Images; p. 10 Flynn Larsen/Getty Images; pp. 12, 20 (peanuts) Shutterstock.com; p. 14 Commercial Eye/Getty Images; p. 16 Adrian Pope/Getty Images; p. 18 © Index Stock Imagery/Age Fotostock; p. 20 (medication) © Erik Freeland/Corbis.

Library of Congress Cataloging-in-Publication Data

Robbins, Lynette.
    How to deal with allergies / Lynette Robbins. — 1st ed.
        p. cm. — (Kids' health)
    Includes index
    ISBN 978-1-4042-8139-4 (lib. bdg.) — ISBN 978-1-4358-3414-9 (pbk.) —
ISBN 978-1-4358-3415-6 (6-pack)
    1. Allergy in children—Juvenile literature. I. Title.
    RJ386.R63 2010
    616.97—dc22

                                2009002616

Manufactured in the United States of America

CONTENTS

4

Ahchoo!

Lily went to Amber's house to see her new kitten. The kitten was so cute! Amber let Lily hold him. Soon Lily's eyes began to water. Her nose got itchy and runny. Then Lily sneezed. She felt like she had suddenly come down with a bad cold.

She put the kitten down and went into the kitchen for a drink. Now that she was not holding the kitten, she started to feel better. Amber's mom said that Lily must be allergic to cats! When a person is allergic to something, her body **reacts** badly to that thing even if it is harmless to most people. Something that gives a person a bad reaction is called an allergen.

Sneezing is your body's way of trying to get rid of something that is bothering it. Allergens can cause sneezing.

Do I Have Allergies?

People who have allergies react in different ways. Some people, like Lily, have mild **symptoms**. They may have red, watery, or itchy eyes, a runny nose, and they may cough or sneeze. Some people's skin itches. They may get a rash or **hives**. These people generally feel better if they stay away from the allergen that causes the reaction.

Some people have more serious reactions. A person with a serious allergy may feel his lips, tongue, and throat swell up. He may have trouble breathing. He may even throw up or faint. People who have serious reactions need help fast!

Sometimes itching on your skin can be caused by something like a bug bite, or it may mean that you have touched or eaten something to which you are allergic.

Springtime Sneezes

It is springtime. Jason's nose starts to run as soon as he goes outside. His eyes get itchy and watery, too. Jason has a kind of allergy called hay fever.

People who have hay fever are allergic to the **pollen** in the air. Pollen comes from flowers, trees, and other plants. Most plants bloom in the spring and early summer. There is more pollen in the air during this time than at other times during the year. People with hay fever will have allergic reactions during the time when the weather is warm. Most people with hay fever are not bothered by this allergy in the winter.

This boy's nose started to run when he smelled the new flowers in his yard. He may not know it, but he could have hay fever.

Peanuts, Eggs, and Wheat

Emily must be very careful never to eat peanuts. Even smelling or touching a peanut can make her very sick. Emily has a serious peanut allergy.

Some people, like Emily, are allergic to certain foods. A person may be allergic to just one kind of food or to many different foods. Some common food allergens are peanuts, tree nuts, eggs, milk, wheat, fish, shellfish, and soy. Most foods do not cause serious reactions. They may make an allergic person feel sick for a few hours. However, some foods, like peanuts or shellfish, can be life-threatening to people who are allergic to them.

A peanut butter sandwich can be a healthy snack for some people. However, for a growing number of people, peanuts can cause a serious allergic reaction.

12

No Bees, Please!

Have you ever been stung by a bee? It likely hurt. A person who is allergic will have a much bigger reaction. Her skin may get red and swell up. A person who is stung on the arm may find her whole arm becomes swollen. It may hurt, be hard to move, and become very itchy. Some people react so badly to bee stings that they must be taken to the hospital. They have problems breathing and other serious issues.

It is not just bee stings that can be a problem. People can have allergic reactions to bites or stings from other insects, such as wasps, hornets, yellow jackets, ants, or even mosquitoes.

People with an allergy to bee stings need to be extra careful around bees. Luckily, bees will generally leave you alone if you leave them alone.

Allergens Around the House

People may be allergic to all kinds of things around the house. Have you ever heard of a **dust mite**? A dust mite is so small you cannot see it without a microscope. Thousands of dust mites live in beds, pillows, rugs, clothing, and other soft, warm places in the house. Some people are allergic to their droppings. Other people are allergic to **mold**, which can grow in warm, wet places in your house.

Chemicals and dyes in some foods or cleaners can be allergens. Some people are even allergic to balloons! Balloons are made from latex. Latex is an allergen for some people.

People who are allergic to dust mites and mold must take extra care in keeping their homes clean. Dusting, vacuuming, and cleaning sheets regularly can help.

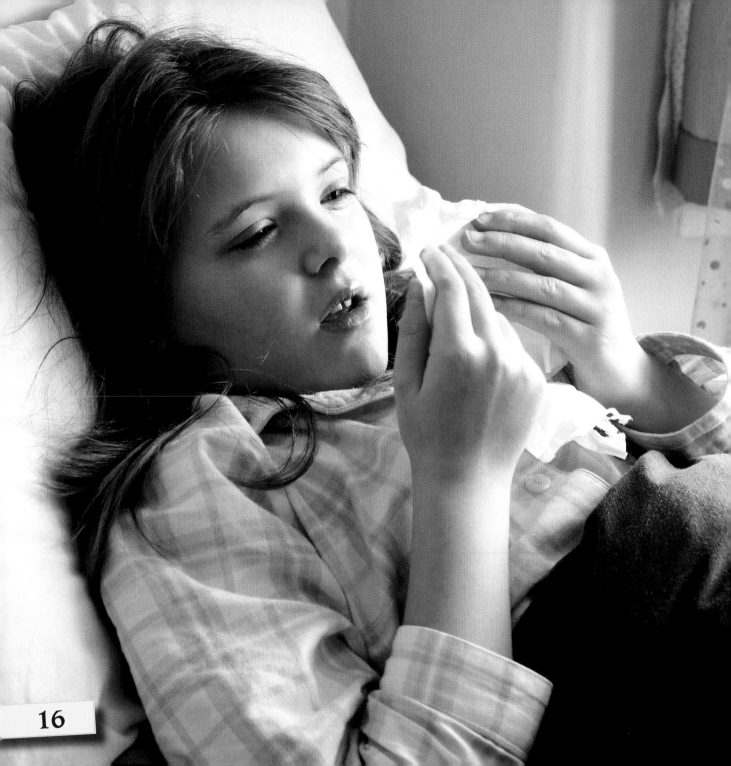

Why Me?

If you have allergies, you may wonder why you have them. You have allergies because your body is trying to keep you healthy. Your body thinks that allergens are **germs**. It fights the allergens because it thinks they will make you sick. Your body does not know that the allergens are harmless.

To fight germs or allergens, your body makes **antibodies**. The antibodies fix themselves to the allergen. They also fix themselves to cells in your body called **mast cells**. The mast cells react by sending out a chemical called **histamine**. Histamine helps fight illnesses. If there is no illness to fight, it causes an allergic reaction. This is what makes you feel sick.

Allergies can make you feel like you have a cold. Your body feels run down, and you may get a stuffy nose, a headache, or a sore throat.

What Can I Do?

Most people with allergies try to stay away from the things that will cause an allergic reaction. That might mean not eating certain foods, staying away from some kinds of animals, or staying indoors when there is a lot of pollen in the air.

When someone has an allergic reaction, there are ways to help him feel better. When Jason feels sick from hay fever, his mother can treat his symptoms with medicine. She gives him pills called **antihistamines** to help stop the histamine from working in his body. There are also drugs for stuffy noses and those that help with skin rashes.

Wash your hands if you touch something to which you are allergic. This washes away the allergen before you touch your nose or eyes, which would cause your body to react. **19**

People who have serious allergies must be very careful not to touch or go near the things that cause reactions. They may need to ask questions about what is in food before they eat it. When a child has a life-threatening allergy, it is important that teachers and other caregivers know about it.

Katie is very allergic to bee stings. She carries an **autoinjector** with her at all times. An autoinjector is a shot she can give to herself. The drug in the autoinjector works fast! Katie hopes she will never have to use her autoinjector. If she gets stung, though, it could save her life!

People with severe allergies to things like nuts (left) should always carry an autoinjector or antihistamine (right). Acting quickly when necessary can save your life.

If you have allergies, the best thing you can do is avoid your allergens. It is okay to stay indoors on days when there is a lot of pollen in the air or to stay away from a friend's pet. It is okay to ask about what is in foods. Make sure adults around you know about your allergies so they can help keep you safe.

It is important to be prepared. Make sure you always have the drugs you need nearby in case you have a reaction. Some people find it helpful to get allergy shots from an allergist. Allergy shots can help a person's body stop reacting to some allergens over time. Remember, many people have allergies. You do not have to let your allergies stop you from having fun!

GLOSSARY

antibodies (AN-tih-bah-deez) Matter made by the body to fight off illness.

antihistamines (an-tee-HIS-tuh-meenz) Drugs used to stop a runny nose and other allergy symptoms.

autoinjector (aw-toh-in-JEK-tur) Something with a needle that a person uses to put drugs into his or her body.

dust mite (DUST MYT) A tiny animal whose droppings cause allergic reactions in some people.

germs (JERMZ) Tiny living things that can cause sickness.

histamine (HIS-tuh-meen) Something given off by cells in the body that causes an allergic reaction.

hives (HYVZ) Itchy bumps on the skin caused by an allergic reaction.

mast cells (MAST SELZ) Cells that make histamines during an allergic reaction.

mold (MOHLD) A fuzzy growth that forms on an animal or a plant when left in a wet place.

pollen (PAH-lin) A yellow dust made by the male parts of flowers.

reacts (ree-AKTS) Acts because something has happened.

symptoms (SIMP-tumz) Signs that show someone is sick.

INDEX

WEB SITES

Due to the changing nature of Internet links, PowerKids Press has developed an online list of Web sites related to the subject of this book. This site is updated regularly. Please use this link to access the list: www.powerkidslinks.com/heal/allergy/